Phil H. LISTEMANN

Colour profiles: Clavework-graphics

Layout & project design: Phil Listemann

Copyright © Phil Listemann 2016

ISBN 978-2918590-84-2

All rights reserved. No parts of this publication may be reproduced, stored in a retrieval system or transmitted in any form or by any means, electronic, mechanical, photocopying, recording or otherwise, without permission in writing from the Authors.

Acknowledgements

J-L Gaynecoetche

Edited by Phil H. Listemann

philedition@wanadoo.fr

Canberra B(I).8
INTRODUCTION

TThe prototype of the B(I)8, VX185, seen on the ground showing the new nose and new shape given to the Canberra. *(Phil Butler)*

The English Electric Canberra is among the most iconic aircraft of the Cold War. Very advanced for its time, it indicated the potential of the British aircraft industry of the post-war period despite a fragile economy.

The Canberra was widely exported, partly thanks to the range of variants built, as it proved such a versatile aircraft. Built first as bomber, it also became a photographic aircraft. English Electric was able to adapt the design to almost any requirement.

The B(I) Mk.8 was introduced to fill the role of a night-intruder flying low level missions in the European theatre and resulted from Air Staff Specification 1B/22D&P, a requirement for a low level interdictor armed with a combination of rockets, guns and bombs. The most noticeable difference between the new version and its predecessors was the raised pilot's station with a fighter-type cockpit canopy offset to port to improve visibility. The navigator/bomb-aimer was moved forward of the pilot in to the nose. A Boulton Paul gunpack, containing four 20mm Hispano 'Aden' guns, could be fitted snugly into the rear of the bomb bay and special bomb doors with cut-outs for the gunpack were fitted. The special doors allowed the B(I)8 to carry flares to illuminate night targets. The gunpack, as well as one 500lb HE bomb (or two 250 pounders) on each underwing pylon, gave the B(I)8 Canberra a definite punch which was used effectively by the Indian Air Force during their UN support effort in the Congo in 1961.

The prototype, VX185, started life as the second prototype Canberra PR.3 hut was then completed as a Canberra B.5. The first flight took place on 23 July 1954. A first production batch of thirty was ordered with serials **WT326-WT348** and **WT362-WT368**. Subsequent orders followed both to provide new aircraft to the RAF but also to replace the aircraft diverted to other nations during production. The serial numbers of aircraft received by the RAF therefore became a bit erratic. The RAF placed another order for 25 (**XH203-XH209**, **XH227-XH244**), then four (**XK951-XK953**, **XK959**), twenty (**XM244-XM245**, **XM262-XM279**) and, finally, one (**XM936**). Exported, the B(I)8 received various denominations: B(I). Mk.12 for New Zealand and South Africa; B(I) Mk.66 for India; B.(I) Mk.78 for Peru; and the B(I) Mk.88 for Venezuela. In all, 72 were built, including seventeen for export and two converted from B2s, but many RAF airframes were later refurbished for export.

The B(I)8 only served with the RAF's Strike Squadrons in West Germany. In its bomber configuration, this mark of Canberra was part of the UK's Nuclear Strike Force and carried a US-made weapon (Project E). Nuclear strikes were to have been delivered by the infamous Low Altitude Bombing System (LABS) technique. This system, developed by the USAF for the Strategic Air Command's B-47s, involved the B(I)8 flying fast and level at around 250 feet then, at a predetermined point, pulling up into a half-loop, releasing the weapon (under clockwork timer control!) at the appropriate time during the climb then letting the science of ballistics deliver it (supposedly) unerringly. Meanwhile, the Canberra would finish the power-climb to the top of the loop, do a half-barrel roll and dive away piling on the speed and high-tailing it for home! That was the plan but, fortunately, no crew had to test its effectiveness.

VX185 taken during one of the test flights. *(Phil Butler)*

TECHNICAL DATA
Canberra B(I). 8

Manufacturer:
English Electric

Type :
Long-range night interdictor or high-altitude bomber

Accommodation:
Two: One pilot and one Navigator

Power plant:
2 × Rolls-Royce Avon R.A.7 Mk.109 turbojets, 7,400 lbf (36 kN) each

Dimensions:
Wingspan : 64 ft 0 in [19,51 m]
Length : 65 ft 6 in [19,96 m]
Height : 15 ft 8 in [4,77 m]

Weights:
Empty : 21,650 lb [9,820 kg]
Loaded : 46,000 lb [20,865 kg]
MTW: 55,000 lb [24,948 kg]

Performance :
Max speed: Mach 0.88 [580 mph, 933 km/h] at 40,000 ft [12,192 m]
Combat radius : 810 mi [700 nm, 1,300 km]
Service ceiling : 48,000 ft [15,000 m]

Armament:
Guns: 4 x 20 mm Hispano Mk.V cannon mounted in rear bomb bay (500 rounds/gun), or 2 x 0.30 in (7.62 mm) machine gun pods

Rockets: 2 x unguided rocket pods with 37 2-inch (51 mm) rockets, or 2 x Matra rocket pods with 18 SNEB 68 mm rockets each

Missiles: A variety of missiles can be carried according to mission requirements, e.g: 2 x AS-30L air-to-surface missiles
Bombs: Total of 8,000 lb (3,628 kg) of payload can be mounted inside the internal bomb bay and on two underwing hardpoints, with the ability to carry a variety of bombs.

Nuclear Weapons: in addition to conventional ordnance, the Canberra was also type-approved for tactical nuclear weapon delivery, including the Mk 7, B28 (Mod 2, 70 kiloton yield), B57 and B43 (as part of a joint program with the United States) plus the Red Beard and WE.177A (Mod A, 10 kiloton yield) nuclear bombs.[155] All nuclear weapons were carried internally.

VX185 showing off its new lines while banking to the right. *(Phil Butler)*

A nice view of a Canberra B(I)8 of 14 Sqn flying among cloud. *(14 Sqn Association)*

No. 3 Squadron
January 1961 - December 1971

Number 3 Squadron was formed on 13 April 1912 and served as a fighter unit during both wars. It continued in this role after the Second World War until 4 January 1961 when it became a bomber unit after No. 59 Squadron was renumbered at RAF Geilenkirchen in West Germany. As soon as the squadron was settled with its new mounts, detachments to RAF Idris, Libya, commenced in May 1961 on a monthly basis. Aircraft used Tarhuna Range for bombing practice while at Idris. In May 1962, the Canberras were detached to Akrotiri for interdictor training and, on their return from Cyprus during the following month, No. 3 Squadron used Wildenrath as its operating base because runway extensions were being carried out at Geilenkirchen. Quick Reaction Alert (QRA) commitment was maintained at Geilenkirchen where the squadron returned to in August. Over the next three years the Canberras were deployed to Malta, Kuantan, Malaya and Cyprus. In September 1965, the monthly detachments to Idris were moved to RAF Luqa, Malta. By 15 January 1968, No. 3 Squadron had completed its move to RAF Laarbruch prior to the closure of
Geilenkirchen.
Over the next few years the squadron continued with exercises and exchanges and during August/September 1971 the squadron had its first detachment to Decimomannu, Sardinia, to use the Cape Frasca weapons range. This was to be the first and last time for the Canberras. On 3 December 1971, the Canberra Disbandment Parade took place. Meanwhile at RAF Wildenrath,
No. 3 (F) Squadron was re-forming in its traditional fighter role with Harrier GR.1s.
During the decade or so the Canberra B(I) 8 was used by the squadron, four were lost in accidents: XM266 on 21 November 1961 (crew killed), XH231 on 3 February 1965 (crew killed), WT330 on 10 November 1965 and XM267 on 15 December 1970 (crew killed). At the time of disbandment, No. 3 Squadron was using XH208/A, XH228/B, XM244/C, XM245/D, XM271/F, XM273/H, XM275/J, XM276/K, XM279/L, WT368/M, WT364/N, XM936/P, WT362/R, WT346/S and WT336/W.

No. 14 Squadron
December 1962 - June 1970

Serving as a bomber and general reconnaissance squadron during the war, No. 14 Squadron disbanded on 1 June 1945 but was re-born on the same day with its number plate transferred to No. 143 Squadron flying Mosquitoes on anti-shipping missions. It reverted to a bomber role when No. 128 Squadron was renumbered 14 at Wahn, West Germany after the former 143 Squadron disbanded in April 1946. It remained equipped with Mosquitoes and when re-equipped with Vampire jets in 1951, it assumed a day-fighter role and eventually flew Hunters. It disbanded once more on 17 December 1962 but, again, on the same day began a new career as a Canberra light-bomber/night-intruder unit when No. 88 Squadron at Wildenrath was renumbered 14. The new 14 Squadron was operational in the nuclear strike and long-range interdiction roles. Although most of the day-to-day flying took place within the low flying system in West Germany, as with the other Canberra intruder squadrons, there were also a number of detachments to bombing ranges in the Mediterranean as well as occasional detachments to Africa and the Middle East. In 1964, 14 Squadron aircraft and crews deployed to Kuantan, an operational detachment that was part of the RAF's response to the Indonesian Confrontation. On this occasion, however, the squadron was not required to take offensive action. It disbanded at Wildenrath on 30 June 1970 and re-formed on the same date at Bruggen as a Phantom strike squadron. Only one Canberra was lost in 14 Squadron service, WT363 on 11 June 1968, and the crew survived. By June 1970, the Canberras in use were WT337/A, WT264/B, WT336/C, WT339/D, WT346/F, WT362/G, WT365/J, WT366/K, WT368/L, WT347/N, WT278/O, XK951/M, XK952 and XM277/P. The letter H used by WT363 lost in 1968 seems not to have been used again by the squadron.

No. 16 Squadron
March 1958 - June 1972

A squadron of old tradition, No. 16 Squadron served as an Army Co-operation unit then as a tactical reconnaissance squadron during WW2 and then, after the war, as a fighter-bomber squadron. It disbanded on 1 June 1957. It was re-formed on 1 March 1958 at Laarbruch as a Canberra light-bomber/night-intruder squadron. The squadron soon worked up to operational pitch in the attack role, training with the LABS for nuclear bombing attacks as well as the more conventional attack methods. It is interesting to note that the Canberras carried a black band around the fuselage that dated back to pre-war days when it was seen on the squadron's Atlases and Audaxes. The squadron flew the Canberra B(I)8s for fourteen years, on the same task, at the same base, and for longer than any other squadron. During that period, as one of the three squadrons of the 2nd Tactical Air Force Canberra Strike Wing (the other two being 59 and 88 Squadrons), one Canberra was always at ten minutes' readiness to carry out a nuclear attack.

Number 16 Squadron eventually disbanded at Laarbruch on 6 June 1972, the last remnant of the Canberra bomber force to be operational, and re-formed there on 16 October with Buccaneers. During the Canberra era, the squadron lost three Canberras: WT334 on 16 February 1960 (with all crew), XM270 on 5 June 1966 (one crewmember lost), and WT366 on 5 May 1971. At the date of disbandment, the last Canberra 8s still on hand and, therefore, the last operational in the RAF were WT336, WT337, WT339, WT346, XM245, XM269, XM271, XM272 and XM275.

No. 59 Squadron
April 1957 - January 1961

Number 59 Squadron was formed in 1916 and during WW2 served in France on army co-operation duties before being transferred to Coastal Command in July 1940. It remained a General Reconnaissance unit for the rest of the war. After the war it served as a transport unit flying York and Hastings aircraft until it became a Canberra light-bomber squadron of the 2nd Tactical Air Force, on 20 August 1956, when No. 102 (B) Squadron was renumbered 59 at Gutersloh, West Germany. In 1957 it traded its Canberra B.2s for Canberra B(I)8s and moved to Geilenkirchen. Part of the unit was detached to Akrotiri, Cyprus, between July and November 1958. On 4 January 1961, No. 59 was renumbered No.3 Squadron and lost a single B(I)8, XH207, on 4 March 1959. Sadly, the two-man crew did not survive.

Canberra B(I)8s of 14 Sqn on dispersal at Wildenrath at the end of the 1960s.

Two Canberra B(I)8s of 14 Sqn flying low during the early stages of their career as shown the black undersides. They are WT336 and WT345.

No. 88 Squadron
January 1956 - December 1962

Number 88 Squadron was formed in July 1917 and it saw service in France as a fighter-reconnaissance squadron. Disbanded in 1919, it re-formed in June 1937, as a bomber squadron, equipped with Fairey Battles. Blenheims and eventually Bostons were later flown operationally. It disbanded in April 1945. In September 1946, 88 Squadron was re-formed for the third time and, for the next eight years, served as a Sunderland flying-boat squadron in the Far East Flying Boat Wing. The squadron disbanded in October 1954. It then returned to a bomber role when it re-formed in West Germany, on 15 January 1956, as a light-bomber/night-intruder unit of the 2nd Tactical Air Force and became the first squadron to receive the Canberra B(I)8. The Canberras carried out their overseas detachments at Malta, Cyprus, El-Adam, Sharjah and Gibraltar. In 1959, the squadron's neighbours were No. 59 Squadron at Geilenkirchen, No. 16 Squadron at Laarbruch (both with B(I)8s), and No. 213 Squadron at Brüggen with B(I)6s. The aircraft rotated around the three Canberra B(I)8 Squadrons after major overhauls at Aldergrove. The Germans called the Canberra B(I)8 'Jaeger Bomber'. The squadron was a close-knit unit and the first all-regular squadron in the RAF after National Service. Like 16 and 59 Squadrons, No. 88 also had United States Air Force personnel on strength. The trips to Gibraltar were to fetch booze for the monthly sherry party.

In 1961, when the newly independent state of Kuwait requested help against a threatened Iraqi invasion - Iraq's General Qasim wanted Kuwait's oil - Great Britain, in less than a week, brought in a mixed force of about 7,500 soldiers with two fighter squadrons, a helicopter carrier and two fleet carriers, mostly from nearby bases, but in part from as far away as West Germany, the United Kingdom and Hong Kong. The Canberras from 88 Squadron went to war and gave support during the Iraqi threat. The squadron flew the Canberra B(I)8 until 17 December 1962 when it was renumbered 14 Squadron at Wildenrath, West Germany. Two Canberras were lost while in service with 88: WT331 on 5 July 1959 (crew safe) and WT335 on 8 September 1959 with both crew killed.

With the snake on the fin, this Canberra, WT339, belongs to 88 Sqn.

Two No. 14 Squadron's Canberra B(I).8s flying low over West Germany at the end of the 1960s. They are XM264 and XM278.
(14 Squadron Association)

The Aircraft

30 English Electric Canberra B(I).8s ordered in February 1951 (as B.2 and later amended) and delivered between July 1955 and June 1956 by Short & Hartland to 6/Acft/6445. WT326-WT348 & WT362-WT368.

WT326

<u>TOC: 21.07.55</u>
Delivered to the Handling Squadron on 01.11.55. Lost before the end of the month by accident, on the 27th.
The aircraft was seen flying at low speed, with the undercarriage down, at a height of 2000 feet about 4 minutes after take-off. It then wen into a spin or near vertical roll and dived into the ground. Squadron Leader **Frank C. COOKE** and Flight Lieutenant **Philip HYDEN** killed. Cooke was awarded the DFC and Bar while serving in the Far East on Liberator with No. 357 Squadron.

WT327

<u>TOC: 31.08.55</u>
Transferred from RAF charge 09.12.55 and spent its life as a trials airframe later on.

WT328

<u>TOC: 31.10.55</u>
Even officially on RAF charge, WT328 did not see RAF service as it was transferred to English Electric (E.E.) charge directly off the production line on 31 October 1955. Not long after this it was again transferred this time to **A&AEE** in January 1956, to be lost on the following 4th May:
The aircraft was being flown on a low level test sortie between St Albans Head and Beachy Head examining the behavior of the radio altimeter at heights of between 50 and 400 feet. It is believed that the pilot allowed the port wing to strike the water whislt turning at low level. The poor weather at that time made conditions unsuitable for the type of sortie being flown. Squadron Leader **Michael R. ALSTON** and Flight Lieutenant **Victor D. HALL**, both killed.

WT328 taken while landing showing its black undersurfaces and white serials. This was the first camouflage painted on the Canberra B(I)8 when they were delivered to the RAF. WT328 was never issued to an RAF squadron.

WT329

TOC: 13.01.56
WT329 remained initially at Warton. It never entered squadron service with the RAF but became a Record Breaker in a flight from London to Cairo on 16 February 1956. After a series of tropical trials at Aden and a stint with the **A&AEE Handling Sqn** it was sent to Boulton Paul for resale to RNZAF on 28.03.58 as a B(I).12 with serial *NZ6101*. Brifley used at **A&AEE Handling Sqn** between 27.07.59 and 27.08.59. Officially struck off charge 27.08.59.

WT329 was never issued to any squadron and flew various trials with the RAF before being modified as a B(I) Mk.12 for the RNZAF.

WT330

TOC: 13.01.56
WT330 first went to the RAF's **Handling Sqn** at RAF Mamby on 04.02.56 for one year and returned for storage at No. 23 MU on 11.02.57. Sent to Marshalls for modifications undertaken between 18.02.57 and 14.05.57 and stored once more. Issued to 2 TAF 04.07.57, and was taken on **No. 59 Sqn** charge the next day. On 04.11.60, sent to English Electric (E.E.) for further modifications, returning to the squadron (now re-numbered **No. 3 Sqn**) on 25.04.61. A brief loan to **A&AEE** for trials regarding the carriage and release of flares between 04.05.62 and 23.07.62, returning to No. 3 Sqn the next day. Sent to E.E. between 18.03.63 and 16.10.63. Issued to **No. 16 Sqn** 22.10.43, then to **No. 3 Sqn** on 05.03.65. Lost in crash a couple of months later:
On 10 November 1965, WT330 suffered engine failure during take off obliging the crew to abandon tak-eoff, overshot the runway and crashed at Akrotiri (Cyprus). Crew safe. Sent to No. 103 MU, it was finally struck off charge as Cat 5 damaged on 18 March 1966.

WT331

TOC: 29.02.56
Initially stored at No. 12 MU from 07.03.56, it was issued to 2 TAF on 01.06.56 and to **No. 88 Sqn** five days later. Returned to the UK on 18.01.57 for modifications and was back to the squadron on 01.04.57. Victim of an accident:
On 05.07.59, while on detachment to Oman, the aircraft strcuk the water whilst attempting to overshoot at RAF Sharjah in poor weather conditions. The aircraft came to rest in an upright position and the crew were able to evacuate it safely.
It was declared Cat 5 (un-repairable) and struck off charge on 14 August the same year.

WT332

TOC: 14.02.56
Initially stored at No. 12 MU from 15.02.56, then issued to 2 TAF on 17.05.56 for **No. 88 Sqn** five days later. Returned to the UK for modifications on 18.01.57, returning to the squadron on 16.04.57. Victim of a Cat.4 accident on 16.12.57, and sent back to the UK for repairs. Stored from 28.04.59 at No. 23 MU, it was issued to RAFG/**Station Flight Laarbruch** on 23.02.60. Returned to E.E. for modifications on 01.08.60, and back to Germany on 02.03.61 and issued to **No. 16 Sqn**. Victim of another accident (Cat.3) on 30.03.62, it returned to service on 08.05.62. Sent to E.E. for modifications on 23.05.63 and upon completion, issued to **No. 3 Sqn** on 27.01.64 (coded M), then to **No. 16 Sqn** 28.10.71. To instructional airframe 22.05.72 and to Nordhorn for fire practice. SOC 30.06.72.

WT332 seen while serving with 3 Sqn (easily identifiable by the green band on the tail and the squadron's emblem located forward of that). The silver undersides were introduced during the mid-sixties and the serials painted in black. The individual letter (M for WT332, see below also painted on the nose wheel door) appeared later on at the end of the 1960s. The letter M was allocated to WT368 in 28 October 1971.

WT333

TOC: 21.03.56
On free loan to **C(A)** two days later and eventually transferred from RAF charge on 13.03.59.

WT334

TOC: 09.03.56
Stored at No. 23 MU from 23.03.56 and issued to 2 TAF 14.06.56 for **No. 88 Sqn** four days later. Sustained a Cat.3 accident on 05.04.57 and returned to the UK for repairs. Returned to 88 Sqn on 27.05.58. To **No. 16 Sqn** 05.09.58 and was lost by accident:
On 16.02.60, the aircraft carried out two dummy bombing attacks on the Nordhorn Range followed by a LABS manoeuvre. The aircraft was seen to pull into a climb into cloud and then re-emerged on a reciprocal heading in a starboard turn and flew on for about one mile in a gnetle descent until it flew into the ground. The most probable cause was that the pilot became disoriented in cloud and in weather conditions which were more turbulent than expected. Flying Officer **Michael J. WATTS** and Flight Lieutenant **Graham G. BYFORD** were killed.

WT335

TOC: 21.03.56
Stored at No. 15 MU between 26.03.56 and 14.06.56 then to No. 33 MU. Issued to 2 TAF 02.10.56 for **No. 88 Sqn** the same day. Returned to the UK for modifications between 07.03.57 and 28.05.57. Issued to the **Handling Squadron** on 30.05.57, then to **No. 88 Sqn** on 11.06.57. Lost by accident:
On 08.09.59, the aircraft had completed its sortie and was returning to base at about 1000 feet. It entered a port turn normally but this steepened to a high angle of bank during which the aircraft lost about 400 feet. It levelled out but then rolled onto its back and dived into the ground. The cause was not positively determined but three spanners were found in the wreckage which suggests the possibility of a loose article jamming the controls or throttles. Flying Officer **David N. MAY** and Flying Officer **Clive A. DEAKIN** were killed.

WT336

TOC: 27.03.56
Stored at No. 33 MU between 24.04.56 and 18.06.56, then issued to 2 TAF for **No. 88 Sqn** two days later. Returned to the UK at E.E. for modifications between 10.07.57 and 30.08.57. Returned to No. 88 Sqn service on 03.09.57. Cat. 3 accident on 03.03.58 returning to service on 30.06.58. Back to E.E. in UK for modifications between 20.07.61 and 10.10.61 and returned to service on 18.10.61. One more upgraded at E.E. between 01.06.62 and 20.11.62. Issued to **No. 14 Sqn** 03.12.62. Cat. 3 accident 18.07.67, being back to the squadron on 02.11.67. To **No. 3 Sqn** 11.03.69 but back to **No. 14 Sqn** on 11.04.69 (coded C). To **No. 3 Sqn** 10.07.70 (coded W) and eventually to **No. 16 Sqn** on 07.09.71. SOC 08.06.72 and to Gutersloh for fire practice.

WT336 of 14 Sqn in 1969-70. Note the squadron's emblems on the tail and nose.

WT336 served in the early 1970s with 3 Sqn and received the full squadron markings. Note the individual letter painted on the nose wheel door and that the serial is now painted in small letters on the fuselage.

WT337

TOC: 31.07.56

Went to No. 23 MU for storage between 02.08.56 and 07.09.56 before being issued to 2 TAF. To **No. 88 Sqn** 02.10.56 but sent back to E.E. for modifications on 12.04.57 and returned to the squadron on 28.05.57. Re-sent to E.E. for further modifications on 04.09.61, then stored at No. 15 MU between 20.11.61 15.02.62 when works were completed. Re-issued to No. 88 Sqn 15.02.62, then left for E.E. on 03.12.62 and eventually went to **No. 16 Sqn** on 24.06.63. On 04.10.65 it was loaned to MoR until 25.02.66, and then was issued to **No. 14 Sqn** on 28.04.66 until 11.06.70 (coded A) when it went to **No. 16 Sqn**. SOC 06.06.72. Transferred to RAFG Bruggen it served as a decoy aircraft staying there until 1977 when it was finally sent to end its days as a target at the Nordhorn air-firing range.

Two side views of WT337 while in service with 14 Sqn. Note that the photographs seem to be similar but note that the squadron's emblems are not painted on the nose in the upper photograph, which was taken in 1968, while the one below was taken in 1970. WT337 is seen landing and showing its silver undersides and serials in the top image.

WT338

TOC: -
Not delivered to the RAF and delivered direct to the Iidian AF as *IF906*.

WT339

TOC: 29.03.56

Went for storage at No. 15 MU on 05.04.56, then to No. 33 MU on 01.05.56. Issued to 2 TAF 18.07.56 for **No. 88 Sqn** 15.02.57. Returned to E.E. for modifications on 15.02.57 and back to the Squadron 02.05.57. Returned to E.E. for further modifications on 13.07.60, being back to the squadron on 20.02.61. Again to E.E. for another set of modifications on 15.02.62 and back to service on 23.08.62. Cat. 3 accident on 05.11.62 and sent for repairs, completed on 24.02.66. Issued to **No. 14 Sqn** 08.03.66 (as D), then to **No. 3 Sqn** on 10.06.70 and to **No. 16 Sqn** on 03.11.71. SOC 09.07.72 and became instructional airframe 8198M at Cranwell.

Above, WT339 seen in full 14 Sqn markings in 1969 and the individual letter 'D'. Below, the same aircraft, taken before being passed to 3 Sqn, with no markings visible but with the serial painted in small letters on the fuselage.

WT340

TOC: 28.08.56

Stored at No. 23 MU until 14.09.56 before being issued to 2 TAF on 14.09.56, then to **No. 88 Sqn** on 25.09.56. Returned to the UK at E.E. for modifications 16.04.57 and returned to the squadron on 13.06.57. Transferred to **No. 16 Sqn** on 18.04.58. On 03.11.60 sent back to E.E. for further modifications, being back to No. 16 Sqn on 23.05.61. On free loan to **MoA** between 02.05.62 and 27.07.62, and re-issued to **No. 16 Sqn** on 31.07.62. Sent to Short Bros for modifications between 14.11.63 and 20.08.64. Returned to No. 16 Sqn on 28.08.64, then to **No. 3 Sqn** on 19.10.71. To No. 7 Engineering Sqn (Eng. Sqn) on 02.12.71 and withdrawn from use on 09.05.72 (i.e. NEA). Sold to Marshalls on 17.12.73 for re-sale to Peru as *251* (G-52-6).

Two photos of WT340 while in service with 16 Sqn. Above, wearing the markings in force in the mid-sixties when the undersides became silver. Note the fuselage band typical of the squadron's Canberras with the unit's emblem on the nose. Below, the same aircraft taken in 1970 with some changes regarding the markings. The serial is painted on the nose wheel door and the squadron crest has replaced the previous emblem.

WT341

TOC: 25.04.56

Stored at No. 33 MU between 27.04.56 and 26.06.56. Issued to 2 TAF 26.06.56 for **No. 88 Sqn** 02.07.56. Returned to E.E. for modifications on 14.03.57 and back to the squadron on 04.06.57. Cat. 3 (but recat. 2) flying accident on 02.12.57. Repaired, it was issued to **No. 16 Sqn** on 10.05.58. Sent again to E.E. to undertake modifications bertween 18.02.61 and 19.05.61, returning to the squadron on 20.06.61. Again to E.E. for further modifications between 16.11.62 and 15.08.63, and re-issued to No. 16 Sqn the next day. Transferred to **No. 14 Sqn** on 09.08.67 but returned to **No. 16 Sqn** nine days later. On 03.11.71, issued to **No. 3 Sqn** until 02.12.72 when it was taken on charge by No. 7 Eng. Sqn. Withdrawn from use on 10.05.72 and SOC on 06.02.73 and served at Little Rissington for fire practice.

WT341 seen in 1969 in 16 Sqn markings in use at that time: black outlined yellow band on the fuselage and the squadron crest under the cockpit.

WT342

TOC: 28.09.56

Stored from 04.10.56 at No. 33 MU. Issued to 2 TAF on 15.11.56 for **No. 88 Sqn** on 27.11.56. Returned to E.E. for modifications on 20.05.57 and was back to the Squadron on 01.07.57. Again to E.E. between 11.08.61 and 18.10.61, and returned to squadron service on 26th. Once more to E.E. for modifications between 03.07.62 and 31.12.62 and issued to **No. 3 Sqn** on 31.01.63, then **No. 16 Sqn** on 18.06.63 but returned to **No. 3 Sqn** on 01.07.63. Transferred to **No. 16 Sqn** on 09.06.66, then to **No. 3 Sqn** on 14.10.71 until 08.12.71 when to was sent to No. 7 Eng. Sqn. Withdrawn from use (i.e. NEA) on 10.05.72 and sold to Marshalls at Cambridge on 08.11.73 for re-sale to Peru as *249* (G-52-4).

WT342 of 16 Sqn in 1968. Note that the crest was present on both sides of the fuselage under the cockpit.

WT343

TOC: -
Not delivered to the RAF and diverted to Peru as *474*.

WT344

TOC: 25.04.56
Went to storage at No. 33 MU between 06.06.56 and 27.08.56. Issued to 2 TAF 27.08.56 for **No. 88 Sqn** on 31.08.56. Returned to E.E. for modifications between 28.05.57 and 28.06.57, returning to squadron service on 02.07.57. Transferred to **No. 16 Sqn** on 10.03.58. Sent back to E.E. on 11.08.61 for modifications, completed on 24.10.61. Stored at No. 15 MU from 30.10.61 and issued to **No. 88 Sqn** on 22.01.62. Once more to E.E. between 07.05.62 and 22.08.62, back to service on 30.08.62. On 25.04.63, sent to E.E. for modifications, works completed on 19.11.63. Issued to **No. 16 Sqn** on 04.12.63 until 10.03.67 when it went sent for storage at No. 15 MU. Sold to B.A.C. on 10.01.69 (G-27-145) for Peru as *245*.

WT345

TOC: 31.10.56
Stored at No. 23 MU between 12.11.56 and 13.12.56 and sent to Marshalls/E.E. for modifications; works completed on 19.03.57 and stored at No. 23 MU three days later. Issued to 2 TAF 25.04.57, then to **No. 59 Sqn** the next day. Transferred to **No. 3 Sqn** on 23.02.61 and sent to E.E. for modifications on 07.03.61. Works completed on 07.06.61 and returned to No. 3 Sqn on 21.06.61. Back to E.E. between 18.07.63 and 16.03.44. Issued to **No. 14 Sqn** on 01.04.64, then to **No. 16 Sqn** on 24.02.67. On loan to Ministry of Technics on 16.06.67, returned to the RAF on 17.07.67. Transferred to **No. 14 Sqn** on 05.09.68, then back to **No. 16 Sqn** on 14.11.68. SOC 23.04.71, became intructional airframe 8197M.

WT345, in the early stages of its career, flying with 59 Sqn which was using a black exclamation mark in an red outlined white triangle (just like the road sign!).

Later on, WT345 served with 16 Sqn and is seen here in 1967.

WT346

TOC: 17.05.56
Stored at No. 23 MU from 28.05.56, then issued to 2 TAF on 03.07.56, taken on **No. 88 Sqn** charge seven days later. Returned to E.E. for modifications between 15.02.57 and 24.04.57. Back to No. 88 Sqn service two days later. Returned to E.E. on 28.12.60 for another set of modifications, completed on 12.05.61. Back to 88 on 23.05.61. Once more to E.E. between 24.10.61 and 19.06.62, then free loan to **A&AEE** between 21.06.62 and 03.07.62 when it returned to the RAFG and issued once more to **No. 88 Sqn** the next day. Transferred to **No. 14 Sqn** with the change of denomination until 07.10.70 when it was passed on to **No. 3 Sqn**. On 14.10.71, transferred to **No. 16 Sqn**. SOC 08.06.72 and became 8179M.

By the end of the career of the Canberra B(I)8, the size of the serial painted on the fuselage was reduced as can be seen on WT346 of 3 Sqn in 1971.

WT347

TOC: 31.10.56
Stored at No. 23 MU from 23.11.56 but sent to Marshalls/E.E. on 13.12.56 for modifications, completed on 06.02.57. Loaned to the **RAE** between 06.02.57 and 01.03.57, then returned to E.E. for further trials, completed on 19.03.57 and stored at No. 49 MU between 21.03.57 and 30.05.57 when it was issued to **Station Flight Wittering** (maintenance undertaken by No. 100 Sqn) until 21.08.59 when it was loaned to **A&AEE**, then to **BCDU** (Bomber Command Development Unit) on 18.12.59. Returned to E.E. on 22.12.60 undertake modifications completed on 12.05.61. Issued to **No. 16 Sqn** on 26.05.61 until 27.08.64 when it sent to Short Bros for further modifications. Stored from 23.04.65, it was back to Germany on 17.05.65 and passed on to **No. 14 Sqn** the next day until 19.06.67 when it was sent for temporary storage at No. 60 MU. Issued to No. 14 Sqn on 13.10.67 until 25.11.68 when it was sent to No. 431 MU, but was back to Squadron on 07.01.69, before being passed on to **No. 3 Sqn** on 16.06.70. Transferred to No. 7 Eng. Squadron on 02.12.71, it was withdrawn from use on 11.05.72 and SOC on 03.01.73. Sent to Catterick for fire fighting.

WT347 seen in 1968 with the full 14 Sqn markings. It was allocated the letter 'N' within the squadron.

WT347 landing with the flaps down and displaying its undersurfaces.

WT348

TOC: -
Not delivered to the RAF and diverted to Peru as *207*.

WT362

TOC: 31.05.56
Stored at No. 23 MU between 08.06.56 and 08.08.56, then issued to No. 2 TAF, and to **No. 88 Sqn** the next day. Returned to E.E. for modifications between 15.02.57 and 30.04.57. Back to squadron on 03.05.57. Between 02.02.59 and 30.04.59, left the 88 for No. 32 MU to undertake new modifications, completed on 30.04.59, then stored at the same place. Re-issued to 2 TAF on 14.08.59, but effective transfer to an operational unit took place on 01.10.59 (No. 88 Sqn). On 09.09.60, sent to E.E. to undertake modifications, completed on 23.03.61, returning to 88 five days later. Sent to E.E. between 28.08.62 and 13.06.63, then issued to **No. 14 Sqn** on 01.04.63 (coded G by the end of the sixties). Transferred to **No. 3 Sqn** on 04.06.70 as 'R', then to No. 7 Eng. Sqn on 02.12.71. Withdrawn from use on 11.05.72 and SOC on 23.01.73, and sent to Catterick for fire practice.

WT362 spent most of its career with 14 Sqn. It is seen here in the beginning of the 1960s still with the undersides painted in semi-matt black. Note the squadron's emblem on the fin.

Two photos of WT362 in full 14 Sqn markings at the end of the sixties. The two images are similar but note that on the upper photo, the engine intake is painted (probably in red).

Eventually, WT362 ended its career with 3 Sqn and was coded 'R'. This photo was taken in 1970.

WT363

TOC: 10.01.57

Sent to No. 23 MU for storage but returned to E.E. between 22.01.57 and 31.03.57 for modifications and returned for storage at the original place between 02.04.57 and 25.04.57. Issued to No. 2 TAF and then to **No. 59 Sqn** on 26.04.57. Transferred to **No. 3 Sqn** on 07.03.61 and sent to E.E. for modifications between 20.07.61 and 26.09.61. Issued to **No. 88 Sqn** 06.10.61. Sent to E.E. on 18.01.62 to be modified, works being completed by 16.11.62. Issued to **No. 14 Sqn** three days later. Cat. 3 accident on 11.10.63 and sent for repairs, returning to the squadron on 06.04.65. Transferred to **No. 16 Sqn** on 23.09.66., then back to **No. 14 Sqn** on 12.12.66. Unavailable between 03.10.67 and 08.01.68 then returned to No. 14 Sqn (coded H).

On 11.06.68, collided with XM268 in formation. XM268 landed safely to base, but WT363 lost its tail in flight. Both crew were able to abandon the aircraft. SOC. 28.06.68.

WT363 was first issued to 59 Sqn and carried the 'danger ahead' road sign marking. Below, WT363 while serving with 14 Sqn at the end of its career, seen here in 1968, coded 'H'. Note that the engine entry is painted as with WT362.

If WT364 served with 3 Sqn for most of the sixties, it received the individual letter 'N' in the last years of the decade. This photo was taken in 1969.

WT364

TOC: 31.05.56

On loan to **C(A)** between 21.08.56 and 06.12.56. Cat. 3 accident on 06.12.56 and sent to repairs, returning to C(A) on 07.02.57 but sent to E.E. for modifications on 02.05.57. Back to C(A) on 31.05.57, it was sent to No. 33 MU on 22.05.58, then to No. 5 MU on 01.09.58. Issued to 2 TAF on 08.10.58, and to **No. 16 Sqn** on 13.10.58, then to **No. 59 Sqn** on 03.04.59. Cat. 3 accident on 24.09.59 and sent for repairs, returning to the squadron on 08.03.60. Sent to E.E. between 14.04.61 and 29.06.61 for modifications, then issued to **No. 3 Sqn** on 03.07.61. Back to E.E. on 28.06.63 for more modifications, completed on 12.03.64, returning to No. 3 Sqn on 01.04.64. Briefly sent to No. 431 MU between 05.09.68 and 20.10.68 then returned to No. 3 Sqn (coded 'N'). To No. 7 Eng. Sqn on 02.12.71 and withdrawn from use on 11.05.72. Sold to Marshalls on 28.11.73 as G-52-5 for Peru as *250*.

WT365

TOC: 15.06.56

Stored at No. 33 MU on 05.10.56. Issued to 2 TAF on 05.12.56, then to **No. 88 Sqn** one week later. Sent to E.E. for modifications on 01.04.57 and works completed on 30.05.57 and returned to the squadron the next day. Sent to No. 52 MU between 23.04.59 and 04.07.59 for other modifications and returned to No. 88 Sqn on 21.11.59 only. To E.E. between 29.09.60 and 07.04.61 to receive modifications and re-issued to No. 88 Sqn on 24.04.61. Back to E.E. between 04.10.62 and 18.04.63, then to **No. 14 Sqn** on 29.04.63. To No. 431 MU between 09.07.69 and 11.08.69 then returned to the squadron (coded J). Transferred to **No. 16 Sqn** on 10.06.70, then to No. 431 MU between 10.06.70 and 30.12.70 and returned to No. 16 Sqn. Withdrawn from use on 16.04.71 and to No. 23 MU for storage and SOC on 08.10.71 and scrapped.

WT365 seen on take off displaying its undersurfaces and serial.

WT365 spent most of its career with 14 Sqn and it is shown here in full squadron markings. By the end of its career with 14, it was allocated the individual letter 'J'.

WT366

TOC: 16.01.57

Stored at No. 23 MU on 21.01.57 but sent back to E.E. for modifications, returning to No. 23 MU on 18.04.57. On 13.05.57, it was issued to 2 TAF and to **No. 59 Sqn** the next day. Cat. 3 accident on 19.08.57, sent for repairs and back to the squadron on 31.10.57. Another Cat.3 accident on 25.07.59, sent for repairs at No. 71 MU between 28.07.59 and 11.11.59. Returned to No. 59 Sqn on 21.11.59. Sent to E.E. for modifications between 30.06.61 and 13.09.61 and issued to **No. 88 Sqn** on 26.09.61. Again to E.E. for more modifications between 13.03.62 and 01.10.62 and sent to **No. 14 Sqn** (formely 88 Sqn), later coded 'K'. Sent to No. 431 MU between 05.05.69 and 16.07.69 and returned to No. 14 Sqn the same day, then to **No. 16 Sqn** on 04.07.70. Lost three months later:

On 05.10.71, the aircraft was seen to pull up into a climb and then to enter a wing over and to dive straight into the ground. Altough initially suspected to be e bird strike or an attempt to avoid birds, no damage could be found consistent with the aircraft flying into birds. An experienced squadron pilot subsequently attempted to repeat the flight and to make the aircraft depart from controlled flight but was unable to do so'. Flying Officer **Keith R. HOLMES** and Flight Lieutenant **Christopher W. KING** were killed. SOC 11.10.71.

Various views of WT366 during its time service with 14 Sqn by the end of which it was coded 'K'. It wears the full squadron markings on the tail and nose.

The last assignment for WT366 was 16 Sqn as seen here with the squadron crest painted on the nose and also identifiable by the fuselage band. Note, on the photo below, the presence of 'The Saint' logo from the famous British TV series of the 1960s.

WT367

TOC: -
Not delivered to the RAF and diverted to Peru as *476*.

WT368

TOC: 29.06.56
Briefly stored at No. 23 MU between 02.08.56 and 29.08.56, then issued to 2 TAF for **No. 88 Sqn** on 31.08.56. Returned to E.E. on 12.04.57 for modifications, works being completed on 31.05.57. Back to the squadron on 03.06.57, then transferred to **No. 16 Sqn** on 18.02.58 and back to **No. 88 Sqn** on 08.09.58. Sent to E.E. on 21.04.61 for modifications and returned to No. 88 Sqn on 05.07.61. Returned to E.E. between 14.10.61 and 15.05.62 for another set of modifications, being back to squadron on 19.05.62 . On 17.12.62 renumbered **No. 14 Sqn** and coded L. Transferred to **No. 16 Sqn** on 04.06.70, then to **No. 3 Sqn** on 28.10.71 (coded M). To No. 7 Eng. Sqn on 02.12.71 and withdrawn from use on 11.05.72. Sold to Marshalls on 25.10.73 as G-52-2 for Peru as *247*.

WT368 served only a few weeks with 3 Sqn so it was very lucky to get a photo of it in the unit's markings.

25 English Electric Canberra B(I).8s ordered in July 1954 and delivered between August 1956 and September 1958 by English Electric to Contract 6/Acft/11158: XH203-XH209, XH227-XH244.

XH203

TOC: -
Not delivered to the RAF and delivered to Indian AF as *IF896*.

XH204

TOC: 08.02.57
Stored at No. 23 MU for one week between 11.02.57 and 18.02.57 and sent to Marshalls to undertake modifications. Completed on 30.04.57 and re-sent for storage at No. 23 MU on 03.05.57. Issued to 2 TAF on 20.05.57 and to **No. 59 Sqn** the next day. Sent to E.E. for modifictaions between 06.12.60 and 09.05.61, then issued to **No. 3 Sqn** on 23.05.61. Returned to E.E. between 04.07.62 and 12.03.63 and returned on No. 3 Sqn service on 18.03.63. Lost by accident:
On 09.05.67, the ailerons jammed causing the aircraft rolling. Abandonned by the crew 8m NE of Wesel, the crew escaping safely.

XH205

TOC: -
Not delivered to the RAF and delivered to Indian AF as *IF897*.

XH206

TOC: -
Not delivered to the RAF and delivered to Peruvian AF as *478*.

XH207

TOC: 12.10.56
Stored between 02.11.56 and 13.02.57 at No. 15 MU then sent to Marshalls for modifications, completed on 15.04.57 and returned to No. 15 MU the next day. Issued to 2 TAF on 31.05.57, and to **No. 59 Sqn** on 03.06.57. lost by accident:
On 04.03.59, the aircraft crashed in hilly country about 50 to 90 miles from its briefed course, striking the ground in an inverted position starboard wing first before cartwheeling and exploding. It seems probable that, having flown in an area he was briefed to avoid, the pilot then flew below his briefed minimum altitude of 2000 feet in order to stay below the cloud which was at 1500 feet and that he subsequently stalled. Flying Officer **Michael J. HARROP** and Flying Officer **Anthony J. S. BROWN** killed.

XH208

TOC: 13.03.57
Stored at No. 23 MU from 14.03.57 but sent on 21.03.57 to Marshalls to undertake modifications. Completed on 19.05.57; it returned to No. 23 MU the next day and was issued to 2 TAF on 14.06.57 then to **No. 59 Sqn** three days later. Sent to E.E. between 25.04.61 and 12.07.61. Issued to **No. 3 Sqn** on 11.08.61. Returned once more to E.E. from 15.12.61 back to the squadron on 06.07.62. Cat. 2 accident 08.06.67 and sent for repairs completed on 23.11.68. Stored at No. 43 MU between 24.11.68 and 30.01.69 and returned to No. 3 Sqn. SOC 13.08.71 and became instructional airframe 8176M at Bruggen.

WH208, after a brief stay with 59 Sqn would actually fly with 3 Sqn for a large part of the sixties. It is seen here in the first scheme of black undersides and white serials (before 1965). No individual letters are evident but 3 Squadron's markings are clearly visible on the tail.

The opposite side of XH208 in the early sixties (see previous page) and below when it returned to the squadron in 1969, now coded 'A', and wearing the new post-1965 camouflage.

XH209

TOC: 31.10.56
Stored at No. 23 MU from 05.12.56 and 04.01.57 then sent to Marshalls for modifications. Works completed on 09.03.57 and loaned to **A&AEE** between 19.03.57 and 05.09.57, then stored at No. 15 MU. Issued to 2 TAF on 24.10.57 and issued to **No. 59 Sqn** the next day. Brief stay at the **Handling Squadron** between 27.01.58 and 12.02.58 and returned to the squadron. Transferred to **No. 16 Sqn** on 03.04.59. Cat.3 accident on 01.10.59 and back to service on 01.04.60. Sent to E.E. between 08.03.61 and 12.06.61 for modifications and returned to No. 16 Sqn on 05.07.61. Sent for storage on 15.01.68 but re-issued to No. 16 Sqn on 10.03.69. Minor accident on 23.04.69 and sent to No. 431 MU for repairs and back to service on 19.06.69. SOC 08.06.72 and became instructional airframe as 8201M at Gutersloh.

Because XH209 served with 16 Sqn for more or less the entire 1960s, it is easy to see the evolution of the camouflage and markings.
Top, the first scheme, with the black undersides and the squadron insignia on the nose (two keys in saltire). Then, in the middle, the undersurfaces are now silver, introduction of the black fuselage band outlined in yellow, with a small squadron crest under the cockpit. Below, around 1970, 'The Saint' from the famous TV series appeared on many aircraft along with the shark's mouth.

XH227

TOC: -
Not delivered to the RAF and delivered to Indian AF as *IF899*.

XH228

TOC: 19.03.57
Stored at No. 23 MU between 20.03.57 and 26.03.57 then sent ot Marshalls for modifications and returned to No. 23 MU for storage on 21.05.57. Issued to 2 TAF 12.06.57 for **No. 59 Sqn** two days later. Cat. 4 flying accident on 20.07.59 and returned to service on 14.10.60. Sent to E.E. between 11.08.61 and 09.11.61 for modifications, completed on 09.11.61. To **No. 3 Sqn** 22.11.61. Returned to E.E. on 30.01.63 for further modifications and returned to service with No. 3 Sqn on 19.07.63. Sent to No. 431 MU on 15.07.69 but returned to No. 3 Sqn on 21.08.69. To No. 7 Eng. Sqn on 02.12.71. Withdrawn from use 16.05.72 and SOC 22.02.73. Sent to RAF Catterick for fire practice.

A long-term Canberra B(I)8 with 3 Sqn, XH228 received various markings during the decade it served with the unit. Top, the early days, with the black undersurfaces and the squadron insignia on the fin.
Below, the last days, with the silver undersides, the squadron insignia at the same position but inserted in the green band outlined in yellow. Note the individual letter 'B' which was also repeated on the nose wheel door replacing the serial usually painted at that location, a typical 3 Squadron practice.

XH229

TOC: -
Not delivered to the RAF and delivered to Indian AF as *IF900*.

XH230

TOC: -
Not delivered to the RAF and delivered to Indian AF as *IF901*.

XH231

TOC: 11.04.57
Stored at No. 23 MU between 16.04.57 and 26.04.57 then sent to Marshalls for modifications and stored at No. 33 MU for storage on 13.06.57. Issued to 2 TAF 23.07.57 for **No. 59 Sqn** from 30 June. On temporary loan to **C(A)** between 27.08.57 and 16.09.57 and returned to **No. 59 Sqn**. To **No. 3 Sqn** on 05.08.60. Sent to E.E. for modifications on 26.05.61 and returned to No. 3 Sqn service on 05.09.61. Transferred to **No. 88 Sqn** on 13.05.62 but returned to **No. 3 Sqn** on 15.06.62. On 06.10.62 sent to E.E. to undertake modifications completed on 20.05.63 and returned to No. 3 Sqn four days later. Lost by accident.
On 03.02.65, while carrying out a low level exercice, it flew into high ground in bad visibility at Gross Freeden, 5m NE of Bad Iberg, West Germany. Flying Officer **Sidney TOWNSHEND** and Flying Officer **Neil J. TOMPKINS**, both killed.

Left, easily identifiable with the road sign on the fin, XH231 is seen while serving with 59 Sqn and, below, while with 3 Sqn in the middle of the 1960s. At that time no individual letter was assigned and the practice was to paint the engine intake, possibly in Flight colours.

XH232

TOC: -
Not delivered to the RAF and delivered to Indian AF as *IF902*.

XH233

TOC: -
Not delivered to the RAF and delivered to Indian AF as *IF903*.

XH234

TOC: 30.04.57
Stored at No. 23 MU from 02.05.57 but sent to Marshalls/E.E. for modifications on the 8th. Then sent for storage at No. 15 MU on 02.07.57. Sent back to E.E. between 26.08.57 and 12.09.57 and returned to No. 15 MU. Issued 2 TAF on 26.09.57 for **No. 59 Sqn** usage from the 30th. Sent to E.E. on 22.11.60 to undertake modifications completed on 27.04.61. Issued to **No. 3 Sqn** on 04.05.61, then transferred to **No. 88 Sqn** on 22.05.61. To E.E. between 21.02.63 and 25.10.63 for modifications. Issued to **No. 16 Sqn** on 15.11.63. Sent to BAC between 04.12.65 and 03.02.66 and returned to No. 16 Sqn on 16th. To No. 431 MU on 22.04.69 but returned to service on 18.06.69. To No. 7 Eng. Sqn on 10.12.71. Withdrawn from use on 30.06.72 and sold to Marshalls on 22.01.74 for Peru as *252*.

Right, no markings visible on XH234 as it taxies during a rainy day. XH234 was issued to 59 Sqn in 1957 and possibly belonged to this unit when the photo was taken. The road sign was applied in the late fifties.
Below, XH234 while serving with 16 Sqn. The fuselage band gives it away. The squadron crest is also applied under the cockpit on both sides.

XH235

TOC: -
Not delivered to the RAF and delivered to Indian AF as *IF904*.

XH236

TOC: -
Not delivered to the RAF and delivered to Indian AF as *IF905*.

XH237

TOC: -
Not delivered to the RAF and delivered to Indian AF as *IF907*.

XH238

TOC: -
Not delivered to the RAF and delivered to Indian AF as *IF908*.

XH239

TOC: -
Not delivered to the RAF and delivered to Indian AF as *IF909*.

XH240

TOC: -
Not delivered to the RAF and delivered to Indian AF as *IF910*.

XH241

TOC: -
Not delivered to the RAF and delivered to Indian AF as *IF911*.

XH242

TOC: -
Not delivered to the RAF and delivered to Indian AF as *IF912*.

XH243

TOC: -
Not delivered to the RAF and delivered to Indian AF as *IF913*.

XH244

<u>TOC:</u> -
Not delivered to the RAF and delivered to Venezuelan AF as *4A39*.

4 English Electric Canberra B(I).8s ordered in December 1955 and delivered in August and September 1956 by English Electric to Contract 6/Acft/6445: XK951-XK953 and 6/Acft/11158: XK959

XK951

<u>TOC:</u> **21.09.56**
Stored at No. 33 MU between 24.09.56 and 05.11.56, then issued to 2 TAF, and to **No. 88 Sqn** the next day. Returned to the UK to underdake modifications between 07.03.57 and 15.05.57 and returned to the squadron two days later. To No. 32 MU 23.04.59 for further modifications completed on 05.07.59 and presumed collected by the squadron soon afterwards. Sent to English Electrics on 11.08.61 for further modifications and returned to No. 88 Sqn on 20.10.61. Back to E.E. between 21.05.62 and 20.02.63. Transferred to **No. 14 Sqn** on 23.011.65. To No. 431 MU on 14.10.69 and returned to the squadron on 01.11.69 (coded M), then issued **No. 16 Sqn** 10.06.70 and No. 3 Sqn 08.09.71. To No. 7 Eng Squadron 08.12.71 and withdrawn from use 30.06.72. Sold to Marshalls 22.10.73 for Peru as *248*.

Taken from a three-quarter front angle, this photo makes the Canberra look very impressive with the shark's mouth painted on the nose. This marking was introduced at the end of the sixties by 16 Sqn. Note the small serial on the fuselage and the uncommon absence of the squadron badge on the nose.

XK952

TOC: 31.08.56

Stored at No. 33 between 26.10.56 and 16.01.57 then sent to Marshalls for modifications and returned for storage on 18.03.57. Issued to 2 TAF 09.05.57 and to **No. 59 Sqn** the next day. Sent to E.E. for further modifications between 06.07.60 and 06.04.61. Issued to **No. 3 Sqn** on 10.04.61. Sent to Shorts for modifications on 22.11.61 completed on 29.09.62. Recollected by No. 3 Sqn 16.10.62, then transferred to **No. 16 Sqn** on 15.06.64. Loaned to **MoA** between 25.11.66 and 31.03.67 and returned to No. 16 Sqn, then **No. 14 Sqn** on 24.10.68 and again **No. 16 Sqn** 12.02.70. To No. 7 Eng Sqn on 08.12.71 and withdrawn from use on 16.05.72. SOC 06.04.73 and sent to Manston for fire fighting practice.

Above, XK952 in 3 Sqn markings, a squadron to which XK952 was allocated twice between 1961 and 1964.
Left, XK952 was then sent to 16 Sqn in June 1964. Note that the squadron's insignia is still there but the undersurfaces are now silver. The large insignia would be replaced by a smaller crest later on. The combination of the silver undersides and large insignia seems to have existed for only a couple of months (see next photos).

Various photos showing XK952 between 1968 and 1970 with the squadron crest on the nose.

XK953

TOC: -
Not delivered to the RAF and delivered to Indian AF as *IF895*.

XK959

TOC: -
Not delivered to the RAF and delivered to Indian AF as *IF898*.

20 English Electric Canberra B(I).8s ordered in February 1957 and delivered between August 1958 and March 1959 by English Electric to Contract 6/Acft/11158

XM244

TOC: 15.08.58
Stored at No. 33 between 25.08.58 and 01.10.58 when it was issued to 2 TAF. Taken on **No. 16 Sqn** charge on 03.10.58. Sent to E.E. for modifications on 18.05.61, returning to the squadron on 11.06.61. Back to E.E. again between 06.09.63 and 30.04.64 and issued to **No. 3 Sqn** on 14.05.64. To **No. 16 Sqn** on 20.05.65 but re-issued to **No. 3 Sqn** on 09.06.65. To No. 431 MU on 13.08.69 and back to service with No. 3 Sqn on 17.09.69, then passed to **No. 16 Sqn** on 19.10.71. To 8202M on 22.05.72 at Gutersloh but SOC 08.06.72 for components and decoy.

XM244 seen while serving as 'C' with 3 Sqn after 1965 and before it was issued to 16 Sqn in 1971.

At the beginning of the seventies, the Canberra B(I)8s had the serials painted on their fuselages reduced in size as can be seen above with 3 Sqn and below with 16 Sqn (the last unit XM244 flew with before being withdrawn from use).

XM245

TOC: 29.08.58

On loan to Boulton-Paul and **A&AEE** between 17.09.58 and 03.12.63 then returned to E.E for modifications. They were completed by 18.06.64 and the aircraft was issued to **No. 14 Sqn** the next day. On 11.05.65 was loaned again to A&AEE until 30.10.65 and was tored. Issued to **No. 3 Sqn** on 22.03.66. To No. 431 MU on 15.05.69 but re-issued to No. 3 Sqn on 23.06.69 (as D), then to **No. 16 Sqn** on 15.10.71. SOC 06.06.72 and used at Nordhorn as target.

Nice shot of XM245 in flight while at A&AEE at the end of the fifties. Below, XM245 in 3 Sqn markings and coded 'D' in 1970.

XM245 at the end of its career with 16 Sqn. Note the small serial on the fuselage and the worn paint of the serial on the wheel door.

XM262

TOC: 19.09.58

Stored at No. 33 MU between 07.10.58 and 18.11.58 to be issued to 2 TAF and issued to **No. 16 Sqn** the next day. Sent to English Electric on 13.07.61 for modifications, completed on 20.09.61 and returned to the squadron on 28.09.61. Returned to E.E. for other modifications between 24.06.63 and 10.02.64, being back to the squadron seven days later. Sent to No. 431 MU on 29.01.69 for disposal but returned to the squadron on 27.02.69. Back to No. 431 MU on 05.05.69, and then returned to the squadron on 02.06.69, then was passed to **No. 3 Sqn** on 30.09.71. Sent to No. 7 Eng. Sqn on 08.12.71 and withdrawn from use on 16.05.72. SOC 23.03.73. To Catterick for fire fighting.

If we exclude the last three months of its career, XM262 served solely with 16 Sqn. Top left, XM262 with the large squadron insignia, a practice of the mid-sixties, and, below left, with the smaller replacement crest.

Nice view of XM262 taxiing.

XM263

TOC: 30.09.58

Stored at No. 33 MU between 09.10.58 and 04.11.58 to be issued to 2 TAF and issued to **No. 16 Sqn** two days later. Sent to English Electric on 25.08.61 for modifications, completed on 10.11.61 then stored at No. 15 MU on 14.11.61. Re-issued to No. 16 Sqn on 18.09.62. Sent to Shorts between 13.11.64 and 28.10.65 and returned to the squadron on 01.11.65. Passed to **No. 3 Sqn** 14.10.71, then to No. 7 Eng Sqn on 08.12.71. Withdrawn from use on 30.06.72 and sold to Marshalls on 13.03.74 for Peru as *255*.

Two views of XM263 in 16 Sqn markings, the unit with which XM263 spent most of its career. Above, around 1966 and, below, in 1970 with the small serial painted on the fuselage and the 'The Saint' insignia on the tail.

XM264

TOC: 31.10.58

Stored at No. 5 MU between 01.12.58 and 03.02.59 when it was issued to 2 TAF and to **No. 16 Sqn** the next day. Sent to English Electric on 05.09.61 for modifications, works being completed by 30.11.61. Stored at No. 15 MU between 04.12.61 and 05.02.62 then issued to **No. 3 Sqn**. Sent to Shorts for refurbishment between 25.03.64 and 27.10.64. To **No. 14 Sqn** on 06.11.64 (coded B). To No. 431 MU 09.08.68 and returned to the squadron on 13.09.68. To **No. 16 Sqn** 11.06.70. SOC 19.06.72 and became 8227M and finally to Laarbruch for fire practice.

Two photographs of XM264 while with 14 Sqn in the second half of the sixties.

XM265

TOC: 23.10.58
Stored at No. 5 MU between 31.10.58 and 02.02.59 and issued to 2 TAF and taken on **16 Sqn** charge the next day. Sent to E.E. for modifications between 16.06.61 and 04.09.61, returning to the squadron the next day. Back again to E.E. for further modifications on 23.08.63, works being completed on 23.04.64. Loaned to MoA (**A&AEE**) between 30.04.64 and 30.11.64 when he was re-issued to RAF Germany and to **No. 16 Sqn** on 01.12.64. Minor accident 10.09.68 and sent for repairs and stored at No. 71 MU between 20.09.68 and 17.12.68 and returned to the squadron. To No. 431 MU between 31.01.69 and 03.03.69 and returned to No. 16 Sqn. Returned various times to No. 431 MU until 1971, eventually issued to No. 16 Sqn for tha last time on 06.07.71. Withdrawn from use on 22.05.72 in becoming 8227M but SOC 06.06.72 at Nordhorn to be reduced to components and decoy.

XM265 of 16 Sqn in the middle of the sixties.

XM266

TOC: 31.10.58
Stored at No. 5 MU between 13.11.58 and 20.04.59, then at No. 23 MU until being issued to No. 2 TAF on 19.08.59. Allocated to **No. 3 Sqn** on 07.09.59. Sent to E.E. for modifications on 04.05.61, works being completed on 03.08.61 and returned to the squadron on 11.08.61. Lost by accident:
On 21.11.61, during a night training flight, one engine failed and the aircraft dived into ground, 2 miles East of Tiverton. Flight Lieutenant **Roger J. MOORE**, pilot and Flying Officer **Martin E.J. ARCHARD**, navigator were killed.

XM267

TOC: 31.10.58
Stored at No. 5 MU between 13.11.58 and 02.02.59 then issued 2 TAF and to **No. 16 Sqn** the next day. Returned to E.E. between 02.03.61 and 19.05.61 for modifications and back to the squadron on 19.06.61. Sent to BAC on 14.02.64 for modifications, completed on 31.08.64. Issued to **No. 3 Sqn** on 04.09.64. To No. 431 MU on 23.05.69, then returned to the squadron on 06.06.69. Lost by accident:
On 15.12.70, while being on deployement to RAF Akroti (Cyprus), the aircraft during overshoot lost power, rolled on and wing hit ground and the Canberra broke up. Both crew were killed, Flying Officer **Roderick C.M. MACMILLAN** and navigator Senior Aircraftman **Kim C. PETTY-FITZMAURICE**. SOC 01.04.71.

XM268

TOC: 12.12.58

Stored at No. 5 MU between 23.12.58 and 23.02.59 then issued to **HQ 2 TAF**, and to **No. 16 Sqn** the next day. Sent to English Electric between 16.06.61 and 24.08.61 for modifications and returned to the squadron on 16.09.61. Returned to E.E. on 27.01.64 for further modifications, works completed on 18.08.64 and returned on service at No. 16 Sqn the same day. To No. 431 MU 19.12.68 and returned on service on 07.02.69, then again to No. 431 MU between 02.04.71 and 23.04.71. To **No. 3 Sqn** 15.10.71 and to No. 7 Eng Sqn 08.12.41. Withdrawn from use 16.05.72. and SOC 08.03.73. To RAF Catterick for fire practice.

XM268 seen while in service with 16 Sqn. Above, in the beginning of the sixties with the black undersurfaces and, below, with the markings adopted in the middle of the sixties when the silver replaced the black paint.

XM269

TOC: 21.11.58
Stored at No. 5 MU between 23.12.58 and 28.04.59, then stored at No. 15 MU until 19.01.60. Issued to RAFG and **Station Flight Wildenrath**. To **No. 88 Sqn** 01.08.60. Sent to English Electric between 12.04.61 and 16.06.61 for modifications. Returned to service with No. 88 Sqn 03.07.61 (*renumbered on 17.12.61 **No. 14 Sqn***). Again to E.E. between 19.06.64 and 28.01.65. Issued to **No. 16 Sqn** 02.02.65. To No. 431 MU between 11.04.69 and 20.05.69 and between 05.10.70 and 24.11.70, returning each time to the squadron. SOC 06.06.72. To Nordhorn for components and target.

The early days and the final days. XM269 with 16 Sqn in 1965 above and, below, in 1971 with the shark's mouth and 'The Saint' insignia.

XM270

TOC: 12.12.58
Stored at No. 5 MU between 23.12.58 and 06.03.59, then issued to 2 TAF for **No. 88 Sqn**. To English Electric between 25.05.61 and 23.08.61, returning to the squadron on 28.08.61. Again to E.E. on 04.03.63 for further modifications, works being completed on 31.08.63. Issued to **No. 16 Sqn** on 03.09.63. Lost by accident.
On 05.06.66, the aircraft spun into ground on approach. The pilot, Flying Officer T.D. Taylor ejected safely, but the navigator, Flying Officer **James V. LANFRANCHI** was killed. SOC 31.07.66.

Photos of Canberras of 88 Sqn are not that common and less so with the squadron's snake on the fin as seen on XM270.

XM271

TOC: 30.12.58
Stored at No. 5 MU between 285.01.59 and 20.06.60 then sent to English Electric for modifications. Works completed by 28.11.60 and issued to **No. 59 Sqn** on 07.12.60. To **No. 3 Sqn** 03.07.61 and returned to E.E. for further modifications on 04.09.64, completed on 29.04.65. On loan to **MoA** between 30.04.65 and 30.08.65, then re-issued to **No. 3 Sqn** on 24.09.65. To No. 431 MU 21.02.69, back to the squadron on 19.03.69. To **No. 16 Sqn** on 15.10.71. SOC as 8204M 14.06.72.

Late markings worn by XM271 while with 3 Sqn in 1969.

For less than a year, between 1971 and 1972, XM271 served with 16 Sqn. At that time, the unit was easily identifiable with the shark's mouth and 'The Saint' on the fin.

XM272

TOC: 005.01.59

Stored at No. 115 MU between 20.02.59 and 19.01.60 and issued to RAFG and **Station Flight Wildenrath**. To **No. 88 Sqn** 01.08.60. Sent to English Electrics for modifications between 20.07.61 and 26.09.61 and returned to the Squadron. Undetook modifications at No. 20 MU between 11.09.62 and 01.10.62 *(17.12.62 renumbered **No. 14 Sqn**)*. Issued to to **No. 16 Sqn** 03.09.63. On 28.05.64, sent to Shorts to be reconditioned and returned to the squadron on 10.02.65. To No. 431 MU between 07.09.68 and 17.10.68 and back to No. 16 Sqn. Again to No. 431 MU between 14.06.69 and 10.07.69 and back again. SOC 20.06.72; to Marham for fire practice.

Wearing 14 Sqn markings, this photo can be easily dated between December 1962 and September 1963 before XM272 was passed on to 16 Sqn.

XM273

TOC: 19.01.59

Stored at No. 5 MU between 23.2.59 and 20.06.60. Sent to English Electric for modifications, works being completed on 14.12.60 and issued to **No. 88 Sqn** 28.12.60 *(17.12.62 renumbered No. 14 Sqn)*. Sent for storage at No. 23 MU on 25.03.64. Issued to **No. 3 Sqn** 14.10.64. Flying accident 02.05.65 and returned to service on 14.07.65. To No. 431 MU 23.10.68 and back to No. 3 Sqn on 14.11.68 (coded H). To No. 7 Eng Sqn 08.12.71. Withdrawn from use 30.06.72 and sold to Marshalls 06.02.74 for Peru as *253*.

XM273 w/n 3 Sqn markings at the end of the sixties. XM273 received the individual letter 'H'.

XM274

TOC: 24.02.59

Stored at No. 15 MU between 27.02.59 and 04.02.60 then issued to RAFG to serve at **Station Flight Bruggen** from the next day. Sent to English Electric for modifications on 01.08.60, works being completed on 28.02.61. Issued to **No. 3 Sqn** 07.03.61. Sent to BAC for recondtionning on 14.05.64 and issued to **No. 16 Sqn** on completion of works on 17.11.64. Flying accident on 21.04.66 and sent for repairs and stored at No. 60 MU from 02.05.66. Returned to No. 16 Sqn on 05.07.66. SOC 24.08.71 to become Instructional airframe as 8170M.

XM274 of 16 Sqn with the standard fuselage band and the squadron crest under the cockpit.

The same aircraft after it had been withdrawn from use. While the insignia 'The Saint' is painted on the fin, the shark's mouth is absent.

XM275

TOC: 06.03.59

Stored at No. 15 MU between 13.03.59 and 01.02.60, then issued to RAFG. **Station Flight Laarbruch** between 04.02.60 and 01.08.60 before being sent to English Electric for modifications, works completed by 02.03.61. Issued to **No. 16 Sqn** six days later. To No. 430 MU 06.09.62 and returned to the squadron on 01.10.62. To E.E. on 16.06.64 to be reconditionned and back to **No. 3 Sqn** on 29.12.64 (later coded J). Flying accident on 11.09.69 and repaired at No. 430 MU. Back to No. 3 Sqn 06.10.69 , then to **No. 16 Sqn** 08.11.71. SOC 20.06.72 and converted to components and used for fire practice at Wattisham.

Nice photo of XM275 in flight while serving with 3 Sqn. The serial is still black but the individual letters have made their appearance.

XM276

TOC: 06.02.59

Free loan to **MoA** between 26.02.59 and 30.04.59, then stored at No. 23 MU. Sent to English Electrics for modifictaions between 29.03.60 and 19.10.60. Issued to **No. 59 Sqn** 07.11.60, then to **No. 3 Sqn** 06.04.61. Sent to Short Bros to be refurbished between 01.10.65 and 26.09.66 and loaned that day to RAE until 30.11.66 when it was issued again to No. 3 Sqn. To No. 431 MU between 29.03.69 and 14.05.69 then stored briefly at No. 71 MU until 03.06.69 when it returned to No. 3 Sqn on 03.06.69. To No. 7 Eng Sqn on 12.11.71 and withdrawn from use on 16.05.72. Sold to Marshalls 18.04.74 for Peru as *256*.

XM276 in the early markings of 3 Sqn.

Unusual photograph showing XM276 while serving with 3 Sqn shortly after the removal of the black paint but still wearing the large white serial on the fuselage. Below, the two sides of XM276, now coded 'K'.

XM277

TOC: 27.02.59
Stored at No. 23 MU between 16.03.59 and 01.02.60 then RAFG. **Station Flight Geilenkirchen** on 09.02.60. Flying accident 19.05.60 and eventually sent to E.E. for repairs, completed by 29.05.61. Issued to **No. 88 Sqn** 06.06.61 *(17.12.62 renumbered No. 14 Sqn)* and sent to Shorts for refurbishment between 04.11.64 and 13.09.65. Returned to No. 14 Sqn 16.08.67 (as P). To No. 431 MU 10.09.69, then No. 14 Sqn 06.10.69. To **No. 3 Sqn** 04.06.70 (as H), and No. 16 Sqn 28.10.71. SOC 23.06.72 as converted to components and sent to Chivenor for fire practice.

Above, XM277 taken after its return to 14 Sqn in 1967. Note the letter 'P' painted on the fin just below the squadron insignia.
Below, the same aircraft later on, with 3 Sqn this time, coded 'H'. This letter was taken over by XM273 on 28 October 1971.

XM278

TOC: 27.02.59

Stored at No. 23 MU between 23.03.59 and 04.04.60. Sent to English Electric for modifications, works completed by 01.11.60. Issued to **No. 16 Sqn** 08.11.60. Modified once more at Batt. A/C Corp between 18.08.64 and 09.03.65 and then issued to **No. 14 Sqn** the next day. Flying accident on 17.12.68 and repaired at No. 71 MU and returned to the squadron on 14.02.69. To No. 431 MU 08.10.69 and re-issued to No. 14 Sqn 05.12.69, then to **No. 3 Sqn** 04.06.70. To No. 7 Eng Sqn 02.12.71. Withdrawn from use 16.05.72 and sold to Marshalls at Cambridge for spares.

It is difficult to put a date on each photo but it seems that XM278 above was taken around 1968 because of the lack of any squadron markings on the nose. Note the 'O' painted on the fin, deleted on the photo below, but with the squadron's markings painted on the nose.

Another interesting point on XM278 is the new style of the letter 'O' on the fin. This time XM278 is in full 14 Sqn markings.

XM279

TOC: 26.03.59
Stored at No. 23 MU between 07.04.59 and 21.03.60 when it was issued to **No. 16 Sqn**. Sent to English Electric 05.09.61 for modifications, works completed on 21.11.61. Sent for storage at No. 15 MU on 23.11.61. Issued to **No. 3 Sqn** 11.01.62 and sent to No. 420 MU for further modifications on 31.08.62. Returned to the squadron on 28.09.62. Sent to Shorts for modifications between 03.11.64 and 28.06.65. To No. 431 MU 18.06.69 and back to the squadron on 25.07.69 (coded L). To No. 7 Eng Sqn 02.12.71. Withdrawn from use 16.05.72. Sold to Marshalls 19.03.74 for Peru as *257*.

XM279 seen at the end of its career with 3 Sqn, coded 'L'. Note the small serial.

One English Electric Canberra B(I).8 ordered in March 1958 and delivered in March 1959 by English Electric to Contract KDE/E/01

XM936

TOC: 31.03.59
Stored at No. 23 MU between 09.04.59 and 16.05.60. Sent to English Electric for modifications between 16.05.60 and 14.11.60. Issued to **No. 59 Sqn** 23.11.60. To No. 3 Sqn 06.01.61. Flying accident 25.09.62, repaired and stored at No. 60 MU between 05.11.62 and 31.01.63 when it was issued to NEAF for trials. Returned to **No. 3 Sqn** on 28.02.63. To Shorts for modifications on 25.06.65, works completed on 21.03.66. Back to No. 3 Sqn 05.04.66. To No. 431 MU 12.03.71, then No. 3 Sqn 07.04.71 (coded P). To No. 7 Eng Sqn 02.12.71. Withdrawn from use 30.06.72. Sold to Marshalls on 11.02.74 for Peru as *254*.

Two side views of XM936 while coded 'P' with 3 Sqn at the end of the sixties.

The Exports
NEW ZEALAND

The RNZAF placed an order for eleven B(I) Mk.12s in 1958 with serials **NZ6101-NZ6111**. The B(I)12 was a B(I)8 with an autopilot and an additional fuel tank fitted in the weapons bay. The first aircraft in the order was a converted RAF B(I)8 (NZ6101, ex WT329) and the other ten were new build airframes. They were delivered between October 1959 and June 1961. They were used by 14 Sqn until July 1970 when the eight surviving airframes were sold to India. The B(I)12 flew about 40,000 hours in RNZAF markings.

The RNZAF Canberra B(I)12 first flew in a Natural Metal Finish but were camouflaged in the latter part of their career. Neither of the two seen on this page were sold to India. NZ6104 (above) crashed into the sea off Singapore on 30 November 1964, killing both crew, and, below, NZ6106 could not be sold as serious manufacturing flaws were discovered in the main spar in 1969 and the aircraft was withdrawn from use. *(via J-L Gaynecoetche)*

SOUTH AFRICA

In 1962 the SAAF ordered six new Canberra B(I)12s which received the serials **451-456**. They were delivered between October 1963 and April 1964. They were put into service with 12 Sqn and used on operations over Angola during the 1970s. One (452) was shot down in March 1979. The five surviving airframes were sold to Peru in November 1991.

Above, No. 456 of the SAAF had the distinction of being the last Canberra built. It is seen shortly before its delivery to the SAAF. Below, No. 455 at the end of its career. By that time the B(I)12s had received low visibility camouflage. *(via J-L Gaynecoetche)*

INDIA

The Indian Air Force became the largest user of the intruder Canberra. India ordered 66 Canberra B(I) Mk.58s in January 1957 which were serialled **IF895-IF910** (all former RAF aircraft, see RAF register), **IF911-IF933** and **IF960-IF984**. The conversion was designated and executed by Boulton Paul. In 1963, six B(I)58s (**BF595-600**) were ordered and in 1970 India purchased the eight former RNZAF B(I)12s. These received the serials **F1183-F1190** to make a total of 79 serving with the Indian Air Force. They were intensively used in various military operations including missions under the UN banner in ex-Belgian Congo and the two Indo-Pakistan wars of 1965 and 1971. Some were lost in action. The Canberra was phased out in May 2007.

Above, IF976 of 5 Sqn, IAF, in 1967. Note the elephant painted on the nose that was the emblem of this squadron. It was the first squadron to convert on this variant and it relinquished the Canberra for the Jaguar in July 1981. Other squadrons that flew the type were No. 16 (until December 1986), No. 35 (until 2001 but from the 1980s was employed in the Electronic Warfare role). Left, IF901, seen in 2001 while in service with 106 Sqn. This squadron was a reconnaissance unit, flying PR Canberras, but, in 2001 a couple of surviving B(I)58s were on strength. Note that IF901 had been repainted in PR Blue. IF901 was also one of the Indian Canberras sent to the Belgian Congo forty years previously! Bottom left, IF922 converted to a target-towing role.
(via J-L Gaynecoetche)

PERU

Peru became the first export customer for the Canberra B(I)8, the order being for nine aircraft, with serials **474-482**, to serve with Grupo 21. Deliveries began in May 1956. In 1960 a new serial range was given, **206 to 212**, which included a new replacement aircraft received the same year (208). In 1974, Peru ordered eleven former RAF B(I)8s and, after refurbishment by Marshalls at Cambridge, they were delivered as B(I) Mk.68s with serials **247 to 257**. Deliveries took place between March 1975 and July 1978. Finally, in 1991, Peru purchased the five remaining South African B(I)12s which received the serials **200-204**. They were used against Ecuador in 1995 and were withdrawn from use in 2003.

Above, Canberra B(I)68 No. 256 was the former RAF machine XM276. This photo was taken in 1995 and the camouflage is a bit worn. Below, one of the five B(I)12s purchased from South Africa in 1991 still wearing its blue paint. No. 203 was formally No. 455 in the SAAF.
(via J-L Gaynecoetche)

VENEZUELA

The first true Canberra export order came in 1952 from Venezuela with an order for six B.2s. Other orders followed which included eight intruder B(I)8s ordered in January 1957. The five surviving aircraft were later overhauled in the UK at the end of the 1970s and returned to Venezuela as B(I) Mk.88s. They were retired in September 1990.

When the Canberra B(I)8s arrived in Venezuela, they were intended to be used by the Escuadrón de Bombardeo 39 based at Barcelona. They received the codes **4A39**, **5A39**, **4B39**, **5B39**, **1C39**, **2C39**, **3C69** and **4C39**. The system changed at the end of the sixties and the surviving aircraft were re-serialled as follows: 4A39 became **3216**, 4B39 became **0923**, 1C39 became **0240**, 2C39 became **0269**, 3C39 became **0426** and 4C39 became **0453**. They were later refurbished to B(I)88 standard and the five surviving aircraft had returned to Venezuela by May 1980.
(via J-L Gaynecoetche)

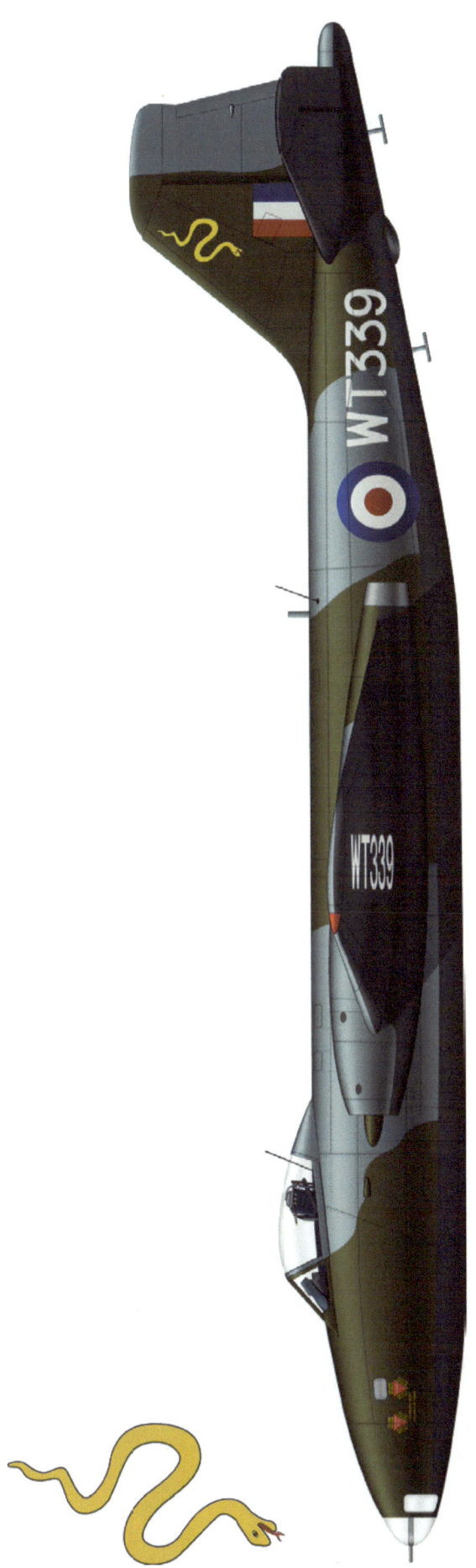

English Electric Canberra B(I). 8 WT339, No. 88 Squadron, Wildenrath (West Germany) 1958.

English Electric Canberra B(I). 8 XH231, No. 59 Squadron, Geilenkirchen (West Germany) 1958.

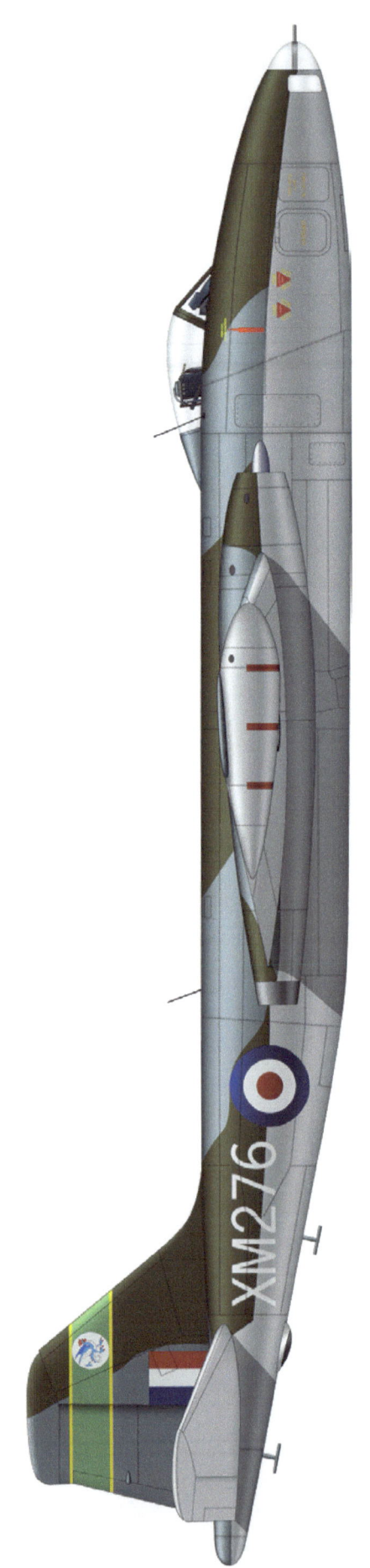

English Electric Canberra B(I). 8 XM276, No. 3 Squadron, Geilenkirchen (West Germany) 1964.

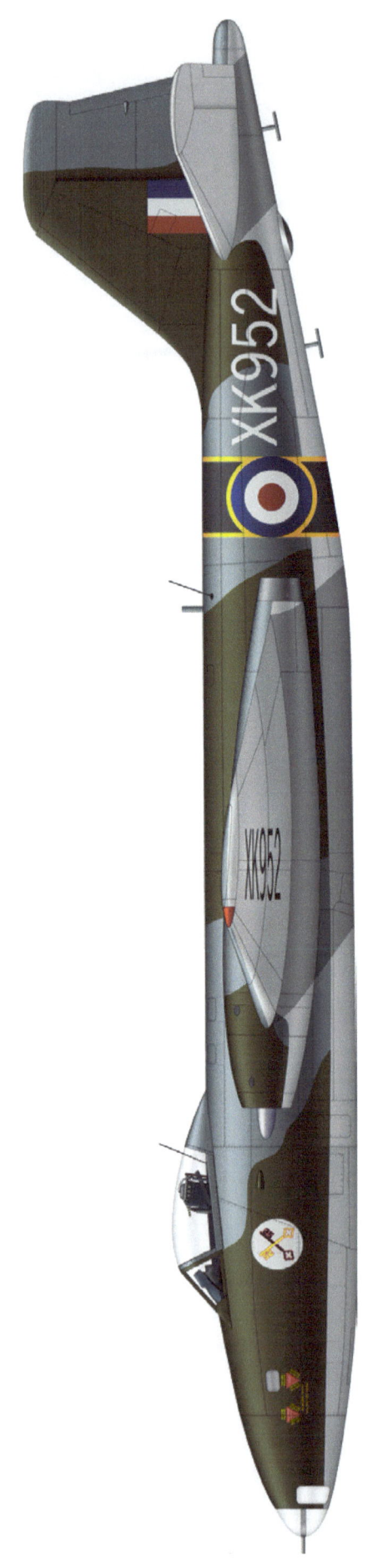

English Electric Canberra B(I). 8 XK952, No. 16 Squadron, Larrbruch (West Germany) 1965.

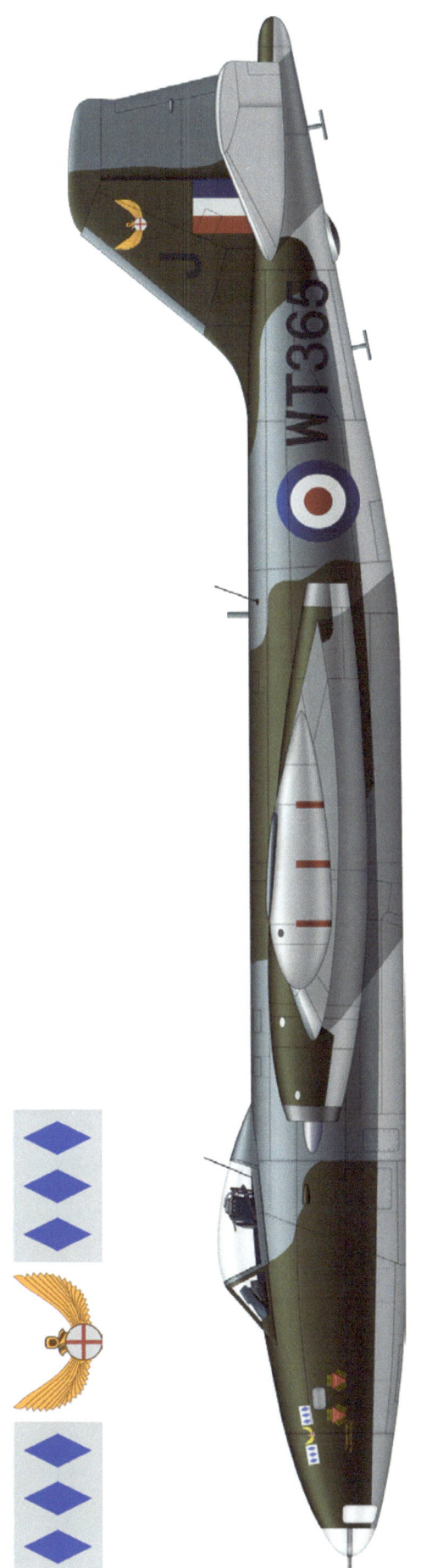

English Electric Canberra B(I). 8 WT366, No. 14 Squadron, Windenrath (West Germany) 1966.

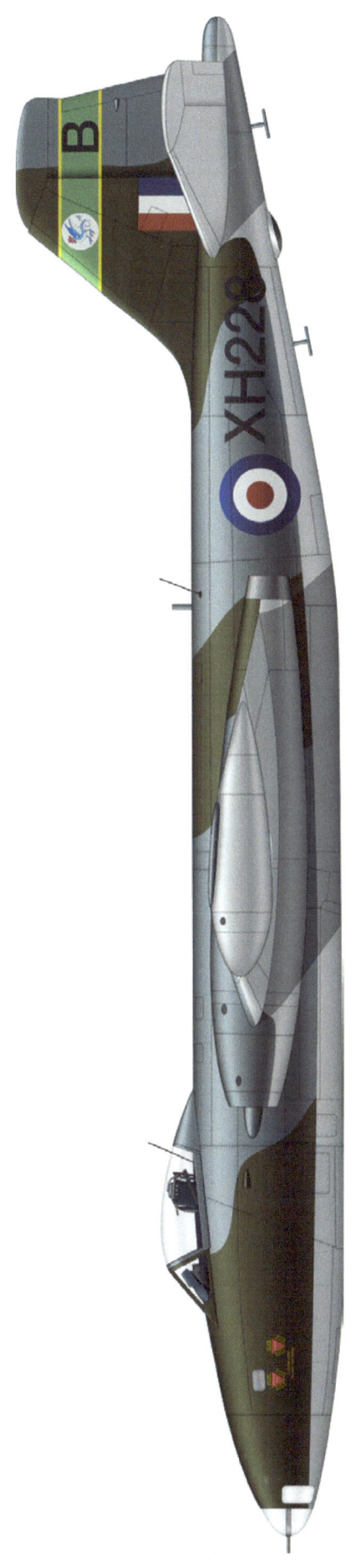

English Electric Canberra B(I). 8 XH228, No. 3 Squadron, Laarbruch (West Germany) 1968.

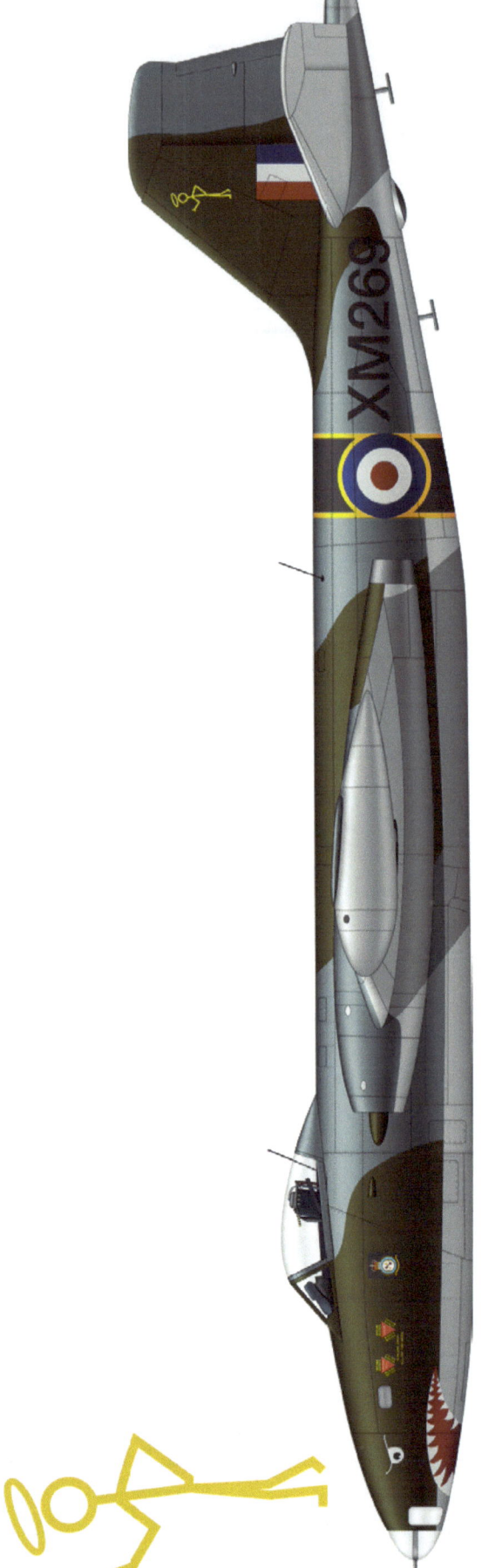

English Electric Canberra B(I). 8 XM269, No. 16 Squadron, Laarbruch (West Germany) 1971.

No. 59 Squadron

No. 16 Squadron

No. 14 Squadron

No. 3 Squadron

www.ingramcontent.com/pod-product-compliance
Lightning Source LLC
Chambersburg PA
CBHW042009150426
43195CB00002B/73